ZOO

ALSO BY ALICE FRIMAN

Inverted Fire

Reporting from Corinth

A Question of Innocence (chapbook)

Song to My Sister (chapbook)

Insomniac Heart (chapbook)

Driving for Jimmy Wonderland (chapbook)

Loaves and Fishes: A Book of Indiana Women Poets (editor)

Zoo

Alice Friman

THE UNIVERSITY OF
ARKANSAS PRESS
Fayetteville   1999

03   02   01   00   99   5   4   3   2   1

Designed by Liz Lester

⊛ The paper used in this publication meets the mini-
mum requirements of the American National Standard
for Permanence of Paper for Printed Library Materials
Z39.48-1984.

Library of Congress Cataloging-in-Publication Data

Friman, Alice.
      Zoo / Alice Friman.
            p.   cm.
      ISBN 1-55728-566-7 (alk. paper)
      I. Title.
PS3556.R5685Z39   1999
811'.54—dc21   99-38766
                                          CIP

for Dale Kushner

ACKNOWLEDGMENTS

Certain poems in *Zoo* first appeared in the following publications to which grateful acknowledgment is made:

Atlanta Review: "Letter from an Empty House"
Carolina Quarterly: "In the Chronicles of Paradise"
Chelsea: "Romance," "The Squirrel"
Five Points: "Wrapping Up the Lost"
The Flying Island: "Crystal"
The Georgia Review: "Under Water"
The Gettysburg Review: "A Little Feast," "The Longing"
Hopewell Review: "The Drawstring"
Indiana Review: "Forgive and Forget"
Iowa Woman: "Unfinished Lines"
The Laurel Review: "The Chicken Flag," "From the Looking Glass," "Poem for Trees," "Mary's Boys," "The Papaya," "Fat Leo"
The Malahat Review: "Matisse's Windows," "The Trouble with Nightingales"
Manoa: "Flying Home," "Ancestry," "Vultures," "The Corpse," "White River"
New Letters: "Honeymoon," "From the Lava Papers"
North Dakota Quarterly: "Speaking of Cats"
Northwest Review: "The Substitute"
The Ohio Review: "Diapers for My Father"
Poetry Northwest: "Storage," "Hymie" (under the title "Mink")
Prairie Schooner: "Confession," "Axis," "Sunday Morning at the Beach, I Think of Mountains," "The Exile," "Nature"
Puerto del Sol: "Even Then, My Mother's Face"
Quarterly West: "Transformations"
The Register Citizen: "Between You, Me, and The Great Wallendas"
Writers' Forum: "At St. John's Monastery," *"In Medias Res"*

"The Squirrel" won the Lucille Medwick Memorial Award from Poetry Society of America, 1993.

"The Drawstring" won the Award for Excellence in Poetry from *Hopewell Review*, 1995.

"From the Lava Papers" was the co-winner of the Firman Houghton Award from the New England Poetry Club, 1996.

"Mary's Boys" (the complete set) won second prize in the Anna Davidson Rosenberg Award Competition for Poems on the Jewish Experience, 1996.

Zoo won the 1998 Ezra Pound Poetry Award from Truman State University.

Various poems also appeared in the following overseas publications:

Abiko Quarterly (Japan), *Cyphers* (Ireland), *Envoi* (UK), *London Magazine* (UK), *London Review of Books* (UK), *Other Poetry* (UK), *Poetry Review* (UK), *Poetry Wales* (UK), *The Prague Revue* (Czech Republic), *Quartz* (UK), *Scarp* (Australia), *Takahe* (New Zealand), *Westerly* (Australia).

The author is grateful to the Virginia Center for the Creative Arts, Kalani Honua, and Byrdcliffe Arts Colony, where many of these poems were written. The author also wishes to thank Lana Osterman, who aided greatly in the preparation of this manuscript, and all good friends who have helped over the years with encouragement, advice, and endurance, especially Marilyn Kallet, Dale Kushner, and my husband, Bruce Gentry.

CONTENTS

IV. *Hunger*

I. Nature

A Little Feast

Baked dogs fattened on poi were the principal
meat at feasts. Puppies were sometimes
suckled by lactating women.

Bishop Museum, Honolulu

Mauna Loa, the world's largest mountain,
spreads out against the windy bolster
of the sky. Not steep-sided like Everest
or Hood but swollen, more mound
than mountain: the floating breast
of Hina—water woman, goddess of seas—
arching her back to freckle in the sun.

When a woman lies down
her breasts spread, slide
in a sweet flop sideways, the nipples
soft in a pout like a girl's again.
The chest bone, the rib cage blanketed
in a pudding, a nuzzle of jelly.
Oh, the big-breasted wahine of Hawaii,
the lovely four-hundred-pounders
dozing in the shade of a banana leaf.
Come 'ilio, little dog, they'd croon,
my pahua, my mother of pearl,
my shark with baby teeth, come
little tail thumper, yapper of my heart.
Lap me with your dangle tongue, purple
as the banana flower, nibble me here
little mossy face, prickle me up
here where I've sugared the poi with milk
oozing in a puddle. Little blind one,

little hungry man.
　　　　　And when they reached for it
crisp on a platter of leaves—mullet,
yam, yellow-fin tuna licked from the fingers—
were they radiant,
scraping meat from between the bones,
cracking a leg, sucking out the marrow?

In Medias Res

In a lawn chair under a tree
Eve woke. Those golden
Delicious, three on a stem
And patient as pawnbroker balls,
Clinked in the always May.
The pangolin uncurled at her feet.
An elephant lowered his pizzle
To start Lake Victoria.
It was the seventh day.
Eve rested. Across her lap
A shadow. Raven—
Stitching a black thread
Into the sky. Eve touched
Her left breast, the meandering
Vein twisting around her nipple
Like a hook.

Even before the Greeks,
Four lions, abracadabra
On a ledge, blinking, heavy
In the sun. A zebra carcass,
Twenty feet away, already eaten.

Vultures

Iron beaks to a magnet, they come.
Circle once, twice, then settle. Spread
their wings into a tablecloth of frenzy,
heads ducked under to feed.
And when they're done, zebra ribs stick up
like fence palings of an abandoned house, all black-
white curtains of decency shoved aside.

But when zebra fall, sick or old, not
run down by cheetah or lion ambush,
but intact, the striped wall impregnable,
it's not what you imagine.

They start with the eye, the one staring up.
One snake-necked Whiteback teeters on the head
then, steady, dips into the socket.
The bird's head, single-minded as a straw,
enters easy, neck down in a bone collar. Retina,
macula, up the optic jelly to the zebra's whole
brain box of pictures. God, the hunger
to feed a crop, to suck out the cones and rods
of grasses, the horizon's steady pull, to bulge
remarkable with another's stash.

On the other end, the great rump,
stilled from twitching flies, lies open as a road map.
Tail fallen aside. Stripes to the right,
the left, pointing the way.
A vulture's head moves in, the beak
careful and deliberate as an oiled glove.

The Samburu say vultures dream
the location of food. Maybe in a dream
you too saw—a ravine, black buffalo
lion-gutted, hyena pacing—and suddenly
stood stunned to watch the hide
fill and shimmy alive again. Not with maggot
or crawly thing, but something bigger. Mother
of nightmare, of hissings and black rags.
Mother of crucibles, Nekhebet
the vulture-headed, draggled with wings.

The Longing

PUNA COAST, HAWAII

I never walked at night
but once. The moon full.
The sea jacked crazy. And I

hanging on to the one scrub palm
at cliff's edge watching the moon
focus her telescope, her pet

beast crawling in on watery knees
then rising against the lava cliffs
only to crash and fall back

seething in a white blood
then gather himself up
like mercury home to its drop

to do it again. I tell you
I raised my arm
making of my hand an eclipse

to stop it, cap the moon
like a Mason jar, gag of wax
and a rubber ring. Might as well

string a hair across the road
to trip motorcycles—this trying
to skid the wheels, hold one idea

high and steady in your mind,
diamond hard and
patient as that palm.

The Squirrel

Her fame lasted a week, the running
tale of the neighborhood. Even after
the man from Central Heating and Air came,
gagged into his handkerchief, while I
steadied the flashlight, held the plastic bag.

We never knew how she got in,
but we knew her terror—knocked-over plants,
broken glass, a spew of droppings on the stair.
Our neighbor said he'd seen her peering out
our windows like an orphan through a fence.
We tried everything, back door ajar,
acorns across the threshold, but by then
we'd heard nothing for days, so we knew.

He had to unscrew bolts, the furnace doors,
pry open a fist of wire to get her out.
In the whole world of the basement
why did she ram herself into a space
no wider than an inch? A corridor to nowhere.
Between two walls. Upside down, swollen and stuck.

The repairman turned away.

Close the curtains. Wrap us in hymns.
Twist in our hands something beautiful,
then burn, bury it, but God, don't open it.
Flesh, sorry flesh, the dirt that dampens,
that smells. Rubbed glossies hidden
between mattress and box spring, our little fat
jammed between the two walls of nothing

that closes in when life doesn't want us
and there's no more room.

On the underside of animals, there is
what feels like a seam. In the privacy
of your hand, you know this.
Vertical along the scrotum, then forward
or back. In women, the short line
between gaps. What did Mother call it?
The baker's pinch to seal shut the dough?
A *bon voyage* from the slip of God's mouth?

The squirrel was pressed head down in a steel suit
with no air or room to scratch the sound
that might have saved her.
And when the furnace man undid the sides
and she slid, heavy into the black plastic,
the body turned and I could see,
all along her belly's length, a faint line.
The darker hairs on either side combing together
the way gears mesh and lock, the way a zipper closes.

Romance

The kudzu that swarmed in June
down to the railroad bed is shriveled now,
reduced to packing hemp and rags. November.
I can see the trees tied in the ropes—
bony, deadpan. The kudzu hissing over them
like bridal veils for skeletons
still waiting for the train.

They're not Redbud, these trees,
or Sweet Cherry or Virginia's White Pine—
three trunks joined at the base
in a bouquet of Graces or Rubens' foamy
mermaids tangling together their hair.
They're no Cedar from a myth, no 90-foot
Shagbark or Lily Magnolia dropping cones
like hankies, red seeds winking from the slits.

They're generic, grow-in-gravel trees,
nickel & dime girls who worked
the counters at Woolworth's
or Al's Diner before it closed, who read
Ladies' Home and *Bride's* then hung around
the depot waiting for a ticket out.

By late spring they'll disappear again
under the waterfall of kudzu. Blanket
of tapping kisses, membrane of love.
Oh happy leaves who must have you
and know you everywhere. The god
in green feathers quivering over you
lowering the shades on a room

of tinted water, a love room.
Who wants to believe
behind all that green whispering—
the grip of tendril, the fingers of wire,
the hiding place of the snake?

Honeymoon

When lions mate they disappear for days,
come together six, eight times a morning.
We saw them on the ridge, he swaying over her,
she on her back fondling his ears, his mouth.
I swear she raked the mane back from his face
and he, intent on nothing but her yellow eye.
Later they'll hunt, feed muzzle to muzzle
snarling in the kill, then lick each other clean
to hold on the tongue the blood taste
from the beloved's face. Such petting.
Such lion love. The sky arching above them—
vast Ouranos heaving himself on top of Earth,
his old girl, glancing over his shoulder
with his bluest eye to copy what he had begun.

Speaking of Cats

Yesterday's leopard
asleep on the bottom limb of an acacia,
the heavy rope of tail hung over the side.
A sign: *At Home/No Visitors.* This morning
we find it, smaller in the dust of the Samburu,
dead. The lions still surround it, bat it around.
One cub plays mouse with the tail, swipes
to make it jump. A male takes the whole head
in his jaws, argues it like a cat with a mole.
We can't look each other in the eye.

Episode to episode, we bounce and
backtrack the Samburu, peering out the windows
like propped up plates in a cupboard.
Zebra ribs lean bloody from a cracked spine,
four lions snarling in the gut. How informed
we are, how pinched and painted our talk.

Five Americans in a bus, behind glass,
in the middle of this vast emptiness
with only a few days left. At least
let's speak of the leopard, admit we also
revel in the stronger, take comfort
in the camaraderie of the bully for the promise
of inclusion. The sure laugh at the foolish
or the one so uneasy in his skin he mirrors
the tongue-tied stranger we're afraid we are—
who's not guilty? Let's talk about the leopard,
we five with only a few days left.

Axis

Somewhere a cul-de-sac dog barks
and the sky slits bloodshot. A few birds
chip-chip halfheartedly at the cold
then give up, seeing the lake, eyes up
and preachy already in a collar of ice.

I sit on a log where horizontal rows of fungi
stick out like white shelves
or seats at the arena waiting for the show.
By 7 a.m. everything is backdrop—
the trees in their sleep, extras
in the storage locker of the cold.
The sky a dirty milk, the sun a grudge.

But stage this at night: the forest
tossing in the joints of sleep, and pulled
from my lamp and book by the whipcrack
of a limb, I drop my cloak of room
behind me and rush out shivering
because I have to see—
huddle on a fallen log, child on a curb again
waiting for the procession. Then—*Now*

wink the briars, red as circus whips.
And the stars jump on their stools.

A rumble low as elephant.
The moon a brass horn. And the trees rise
older than Rex, cradling fog in their arms,
passing it limb to limb like a long chiffon
or the ghost of a never-ending baby,

each fingering as it goes by
grieving for the stem of her own. What's this
but axis: pin of the pinwheel, Fat Maeve laughing,
the heart flailing around its knife?

Nature

The earth has started her
October tilt. By late afternoon
the sun, pushed over the edge,
slides his long fingers
from between the legs of trees
like a practiced human lover
who knows, even to the last gesture,
how to leave—fingertip to fingertip—
as if he could not bear it.

Emerson was right. Nature is
our mirror, bark naked
or itchy with flowers.
Trouble is, suspended in our hammock
between two maples weeping down
our pretty deaths, we prefer
reflections we can sleep with.

In Tanzania, the Bearded Vulture
digests only bones. He tips his head
and knocks back a splintered tibia
left over from last Thursday's wart hog,
gulping it down in inches
like a snake dining on his weekly rat.

What do we make of that, Ralph Waldo?
The clean-plate theory of philosophy?
The earth as restaurant?
God's in his kitchen and all's right
with this butcher block of a world?

From the Lava Papers

To the missionaries who came, hot as Ahab
harpooning for souls, the Hawaiians were sweet meat,
baked dog fattened on poi.
The trap, the net, the sharpened bait stick,
nothing could stop them. Even Maui
who wrestled the birdwoman of the underworld.

From the caldera of Kilauea down to the sea,
the earth rolls in her mouth a phlegm of magma,
unlocks the scroll of her long black tongue.
Each flow—black slabs four feet thick
on top of the last. Far as the eye can see—
nothing but the oozing nightmare of the heart.

In the name of the Word reborn on alien lips,
the missionary swung his cage of fire, walked
in the holy steam. His cassock, black
as morning lava cooled from the night's flares.
Here was Dante's inferno. Here, the new god—
influenza in a pocket, pox sprinkled from his hand.

In the periodic drifts of destruction
what remains? What guilt-stinking bone
needs new clothes, a new excuse to wear them?
Read from the Book of Awe. Turn the pages of rock.
Cave walls, omphalos stone, twin tablets
of Sinai, the Book of the Dead, Church—rock and crown.

Now, the missionary's fist
blooms with ready cash. Lovely hula hands
slosh tables at McDonald's. And Oahu,
big as taro patch, lovely as fishpond, strangles

in a net of military installations, ten of them,
breeding jets like kites that scream over Waikiki,
tipping wings to Diamond Head—that dead crater,
necklace of bunkers, prophecy of stone.

Help Wanted on the Westbound Train

In old Hawaii the bones of kings
were preserved for veneration.
Priests or lesser chiefs, wrapped
in beaten tapa before deposited
in caves. But ordinary you or me—
bound, trussed like a chicken
then cannonballed into a pit.

So who promised fair?
And if Mr. Lilac in a ratty coat
lulled us with democracy in death,
what about the orthopedic nightmare
left at the bottom of the cliff?
Or our specialty—bodies
tumbled weightless without even
the radiance of ceremony, just pieces,
a hip an arm glancing off the plow
like so much rubbish bulldozed into a ditch.

Where's the poet
who makes his home here with us
in the tunnels of rattle
where all talk is misunderstanding
and mouths crimp from the exercise? The one
able to clutch our morning to his chest
like a pawn ticket for a promise
after looking out our dirty windows.
An Orpheus capable of valentines
while dashing, one side of this train
to the other, spitting on his handkerchief,
rubbing circles on the glass.

The Corpse

Somewhere
under last night's shroud of snow,
the dead bird I walked past for a week
flat on her back between College Avenue and Park.
Head to one side, clamped beak, flesh
shrinking into the sinkhole of an eye.

A starling
knocked out by the lottery—BB
or the love bite of a cat, so roundly perfect
the wound, so straight for the heart.
If it were June, a chest hole
for ten thousand ants to glisten in
(bark moving on a branch)
you'd swear the chest was breathing.

Now the snow
draping trees in a white bunting,
kinder in indifference than the Mr. and Mrs.
whose picture window and lamp examined
that sidewalk for a week, the couple who couldn't
slip her decent into black plastic for pick-up.
Kinder than the wind raking his dog teeth,
backcombing feathers to look. And me, kinder than me
nudging with a boot, taking notes, itchy
as an undertaker's apprentice
to paint, embellish, jack things up.

In the Chronicles of Paradise

They'll say
We were in the business
Of killing ourselves off.

In the riches of tadpoles
Among the emeralds of fortune
We tapped our feet for the bandleader
And passed the hat.

You don't believe me?
The cypress has fallen among its knees.
Blond-eyed birds bawk-bawk from the branch.
It is the finest moment of your life.
Wear a tie.

The Drawstring

Pale green and warty,
the autumn fruit of the old bayberry
emerges, covered with a blue-white wax
like vernix. Cobwebs clinging to a new thing.
A shroud for the baby.

In the pucker of a drawstring bag
all ends pull together:
the kiss of beginning touches the end
and deepening lines around the mouth
whimper on a milky kiss. Over the old face
a birth cry hovers.

In yesterday's morning sky, clouds like sheep
spread out from the hole the sun burnt through.
And you and I in a white car, freshly waxed
and beginning like the bayberry in November.

But today, changing the furnace filter,
I found the panic we heard rustling
under the feet of our autumn comfort:
the skull of a tiny bird
offering in a fist of fire its charred
body of feathers. Blossom of carbon.
Anonymous black rose.

It crumbled in my hand.

Even in the basement of my ignorance,
what string of reason through an empty hem
do I pull now—black petals at my feet,
those eye holes, bone holes, watching?

The Trouble with Nightingales

I wake to mourning doves
coo coo cooing their presentiments.
They know, begin each day by knowing
then hush up.

Might as well find an alley to kick a stone.

In a painting once I fell in love
with a gravel walk, rose garden
sun-soaked to the frame.
I shall live here I said,
propped it up in front of my chair.

Two days
and the slanted brushstrokes
darkened into bullets of rain
even before a cloud to put them in
and all I saw were wet roses
bloody in their diagonal hair and me
rattling the locked door of the summerhouse.

I left the painting behind.
Now I shop for one that fits.
No shivering leaves flirting with themselves
in a pond, no saints around a board
blessing their little slice of sunbeam in a dish,
no Venus coasting in on the half shell
delivering our favorite poppy between her thighs.
No pretty, no comfort, no language
without tooth or yell, without hornets
or the old stink of creosote in the yards.

Sweet John of the Odes, for me
nightingales don't visit.
Only this mournful coo coo cooing
coming through the window. Sing me a stanza
to put it in, of stubble and bare trees,
of dry rooms and January, the murmur
of the brain buried in blizzard—
poor paperweight on a neck—watching
and listening through its glass bubble
for any immortal thing.

II. Mary's Boys

Sometimes sixty years go down
same as loose pebbles in a hole.
And when you dig them up—
a queen's abacus, sense on a string.

Mary's Boys

1.

The uncles are dying. Hymie first,
now Jack (Jakey she called him).
My father next, then fat Leo, the baby,
sucking an ulcer for 64 years since he was 12.

She's signaling from under the ground,
blowing the whistle she wore around her neck
in the home to summon the nurses: tangled elastic,
cottage cheese and peaches fed from a plastic tray.
Bent double, inching her walker, 99 years old
and still in high heels. The imperial whistle.
Mary. Maryasha. Queen of all the Russias.
Czarina in a pine box.

Her sons always knew where they belonged.
Wives had nothing to do with it.
Hymie arranged to have himself crated home
in a Delta's belly. Leo's there already,
practicing in his lounge chair 20 minutes away.

That's what she wanted, made them want
from the beginning: laid out like a Passover plate—
a circle of hard-boiled eggs around an old bone.
Her jewelry, her necklace of sons.
That fiction, string enough to hold them.

Only my father, the oldest, will be out of it
the way he always was, butt of jokes, put down
in Florida's insubstantial sand, away
from the family dirt, the dirt he keeps

under his fingernails, refusing to cut them
although Mother harps, handing him the clippers
every Saturday morning after his shower,
each fingernail a child's bank, a piggy's bank—
dirt of the chicken house, his mother, home.

2. Jack

Before he died he wrote kind letters
glorifying his mother—
this man who'd park his car
on someone's grave.

We kept our distance.
It wasn't pity held us back—
the pathetic stamp—but the wonder of it.
Jack Jack the crackerjack turned mellow,
yellow as the cancer that flickered
then glowed on the dead-end wall.

Only his oldest brother understood,
stuck 87 years in the squabbling circle
around his mother's chair.

On the telephone, two old men
smaller than their skins, hooking
their voices through to knit a past
that never was: row after purled row
of years head-tucked and blind.
For weren't they still Mary's boys
with her strut and that straight back?
And hadn't the sun shone on Jakey
in the playing fields, the red
helmet of his hair? What difference
their own children bruised as berries,
the red smears of their lives?

In her last years
when glaucoma pulled her world
through the wrong end of a telescope
and she listened to his bright shape

solicitous at the tube's end, her son
the lawyer, star of her element and will,
she never knew that everything she owned
had slipped into his payments and disappeared.

3. Hymie

Mink

You knew you were twelve
when Uncle Hy offered to teach you
to box. Girl, boy, no difference.
His kids said he could lift a freezer
and you'd believe it, watching him
slam out in boots, stinking of mink feed
and Dobermans. One hour in a locked pen
was all it took to beat a dog into a wall
of slather, trained to chew off car doors.
You were supper cringing in a can, Alpo
with shoes, if the Big Man didn't bark,
call off his hounds.
                              But he could dance.
Made a show of the two-step, spinning
his tiny wife, lifting her giggling
off her feet. A doll, part of their bargain,
even when he'd bait her with "blonde" stories,
models invited to the mink ranch for picnics,
perfumed in money and Grace Kelly polish
so she'd know how lucky she was.
                                    After he died
his kids swore he'd been true-blue.
Maybe families forget what they have to
like the boxing gloves waiting in the closet,
regulation size, you could hardly keep
your arms up—and him tap tapping at your chin
like a metronome, like a time bomb, punching
and jabbing for the crown, the purple trunks,
the blondes, the whole American ticket
wrapped in mink and hanging on a right hook
cocked to let you have it

because that day you were all he had.
Why else did he shoot the horse—dig a hole
the size of a Pontiac and topple her in it
while his kids were at school?

4. Fat Leo

His mama said he happened
at the Dew Drop Inn, Long Branch, N.J.,
where she'd forgotten the little plugs
of cocoa butter rolled at the kitchen table
after her 3 boys were asleep then hid
behind cheese in the icebox.
Eleven years younger than the rest, skinny,
lank hair & an ulcer, the family hole
he stuffed with rugulach & rafts of French toast
pyramided with sugar *to grow hair on your teeth*
he'd say. *My favorite* she'd say. But it was
15-year-old Hymie muscled him into bed,
wiped his vomit, owned him later
with his checkbook. Even the year
baby hit 26 & eloped with the bowling queen,
a gutter ball with big hips. The one time
he bucked his brother & he ran away to do it.
How else to get past him, jealous bull
snorting in the doorway? *She's got no breasts.*
What kind of girl is that?

Now, the bull is dead. Long live the bully!
Wider than an airplane seat, self-crowned
Napoleon of traffic, of funerals
& firemen & flares. His walls bragging
plaques & knight-errant certificates
of disaster. Leo Leo Leo. And why not?
Trailing behind, playing catch-up,
imitating a brother who imitated John Wayne,
what's left to boss, his children gone, but cars,
living 76 years in a brother's pocket,
turning himself into a plug of fat
to fill the angry hole at the bottom of everything.

5. Joseph

She named him
Joseph
but called him Georgie.
Even at the end,
99 & blind, *Georgie*
as if once upon a time, once
she folded her winning hand
crowned by the queen of clubs
to take him up, sick baby,
& rock him, arms around
a wound. Who will sing
the song for Georgie, kicked out
at 14 to bloody his head
against the door? Joseph
who howled all his life
for his mother,
who made his wife into
his mother. His daughters—
his sins, his siblings,
his dingy water, his used goods.
An old man who spits
& rages from habit, banging
with his cane. Who's left
to remember Georgie?
Whose job is that?
I hold a lamp to the mirror.
The old grit still floats,
jabs at the silvered eye
& all that comes out, look—
this sorry skeleton,
this clotted streak, dirty

& skinny down the page
with no fat, no kindness
left. Joseph.
Father.

III. Wrapping Up the Lost

Transformations

Each morning I get reborn as Jack
waking to what sleep grew in the garden.
A tangle of olona and banana trees and always
the soft slapping of rain. My resident spider
sways in the silk grocery of her wheel,
weaving another language than what I know,
and I am Jack, priest of bitten fingernails,
before the beckoning vine.

This morning I'm pulled to the sea
then east on 137 to sit by the graves.
Across the road, six mammoth trees
press to the berm, each draped
in a yellow veil of vines, more veins
than vines. Venae cavae with nothing in them.
Six monoliths, terrible birdless things,
and crowding behind, twelve more. A crush

of giants, of prehistoric brides, captives
of the Laestrygonians, shrouded in a purdah
dark as the forbidden closet door
Mother undressed behind. A funeral of mothers,
dragging their roots through dirt for fifty years
to reach the road, then stopped
as if tar not blood were the river of aching
separating the living from the dead. And I know

I have traveled halfway around the world
to look on this. A sorrow above the brim.
My family storybook
retold in a copse of mango trees

mourning in the prison of their own veins
yanked out because they couldn't bear them beating
then hung where each must watch what should be loved
tap and tap against it looking for a door. Here

is my opening in the clouds, the key
to the ogre's house and his wife's closet
where I hid and never got found. Here
in each fee-fi-fo-fum that drained the blood
out of every dinner. In my sister's misery.
In Mother's wedding clock tolling its pinched rhetoric
in the hall. Here is my golden goose,
my stash of coin. Here is the harp that sings.

Wrapping Up the Lost

LAVA TREE STATE PARK, HAWAII

I write of disappearances: Isabella of Palermo, saint,
stuffed in an iron maiden. And when the boys in hoods
with pincers and other dangling hardware opened it—
not a trace. What they were betting on was a waffle
or mattress with holes ready for the buttons.
Where were the holy bloomers, the teeth?
Then there's my second cousin, Aunt Fanny's boy.
Stepped out to fetch his brown tweed from the cleaner.
Disappeared from the front stoop. Twenty years later
he's dealing blackjack in Vegas. And Nick the hero,
gurgling love in a Long Island telephone booth, 1968.
Went right through the 10¢ slot, never heard from again.

Here on the Big Island, as far from travel-folder Eden
as you get, whole towns disappear. Schools, gas pumps,
the local D.Q. No one knows where they go. Kalapana,
Kapoho, Kamoamoa. All K's. The Kafka connection. Names
still printed on maps in hopes they'll come back, wake up,
fling off their blankets of lava, go about their business.
Not like poor Aunt Fanny, filed her hurt under capital S
for Stroke-waiting-to-happen. Never mentioned baby again.

Better to hold the missing like the vaporized of Pompeii—
2000 years in a cuddle of ash. Or these 'ohi'a trees,
gone but remembered in black hugs of lava. Maybe we too
should make ourselves into molds, walk the streets, arms out
and empty, wrapped around the lost. Imagine New York City,
sidewalks of lawyers and hooligans gently maneuvering

their bundles of ghosts. Everyone a Fred Astaire.
I like to think even the iron maiden, locked each night
in the supply closet, gingerly meshed its crocodile teeth,
creaking out an elegy for the airy one, shot *a cappella*
past the worm's iron grip to where the faded are.

Ancestry

for Yusef Komunyakaa

My great-grandfather
didn't come from Trinidad.
He ran away from Shklov,
another holocaust, halfway
between Minsk & Smolensk
then south on the old road.
But a rubber stamp on Ellis Island
fixed him up. *You can't be*
American with a name like that.
Two wives he had. The Beauty
left in the dirt of Belarus,
pulled down by tuberculosis,
a blind daughter & 11 children
before 40. The second,
a widow woman arranged for
in America who cooked. Dependable
as an iron stove. Her skin, soupy
as boiled chicken. So what.
She was saint in any language, crowned
by asthma, dusting another woman's
claw & ball in a shut-in house.
A good woman. That's all he'd say,
damning with a rusted tongue.
What did he give her but stories
of a dead wife & the use of a kitchen,
another Pale to live in, the rut
of linoleum between sink & stove?
Allowed to shop but not to pay—
the butcher, the egg & cheese man,

Louie's Fish—debts he'd wipe out
once a week, man to man with a flourish.
He even bought her bloomers for her.
I like to think she laughed
watching from the kitchen window—
2 bearded gabardines
haggling over a pushcart,
stealing time from their phylacteries,
their books, their holy scraps,
to rummage in the silky piles, debating
elastic or crotch, swaying & mumbling
over the soft pink mysteries. I want
to think Beauty in her stiff black dress
laughed with her, hanging on their bedroom wall
in her oval frame.

Between You, Me, and The Great Wallendas

After bibbling his lips
my cousin would stick out his tongue
then turn it 360° around.
My sister could clasp her hands
and jump rope with her arms. Even I
could do a trick behind my back—
twisting one arm, making the shoulder
roll out of its socket. We were
the shining ones. Die Wunderkinder.
A nickel a peek.

Growing up, I yawned
into the middle class: *TV Guide*
and coupons for toilet paper and Tide.
My heart murmur, that slushy valve
and sweet excuse from gym, clicked shut
with my high school diary.

Even in bed, when I kiss the two
rose petals on my husband's chest, we drift
dreamy as starfish in a tide pool. Dammit,
I nurse us both to sleep. Where's

bucktoothed Aunt Sadie when you need her?
She told fortunes with cards, peed
with the bathroom door open, her woolies
dropping a bunting between her knees.
Where's Uncle Max? Where's Benny from Shklov
dancing the kozotsky in a Persian lamb hat,
or Aunt Bella, the original fat lady,
sixty-six years in pink and sausage curls,
perched on the edge of Mother's Windsor chair
fiddling the bristles on her chin? O America!

Even Then, My Mother's Face

June 1922. A rented boat.
Saturday. And four of them
at Rockland. Herbie, Frances,
and She, looking serenely out
at the bent head of the boy
pointing the camera, seeing
in that raw package of cowlick
and rage, her opus,
her gold star,
her death do you part.
Sixteen, and already a heroine
to a Cyrano whose lines could never
be more than *cheese* and counting,
a hero so bewitched he bellowed
to fit the triangle they made
into the red slit of his eye.

She must have practiced that look
the way girls do after poetry,
or towel-wrapped in the haze
of bathroom mirrors when they think
they see the bride. I see her
setting the table—middy blouse,
navy pleated skirt—rehearsing
to a spoon the face of forgiveness
in advance—dirty dishes,
grease, the smears on the blade.

If Love perched the gunwales
that day, trailing his golden foot
in the water, it was for Herbie—
cap on backwards the way boys do now,

grinning, the wind flip-flopping his tie
towards Frances beside him on the bench,
her hands, two white birds on the oar.
While She, star of a bigger story,
blazes above them, all high serious
like the Virgin in a Raphael, rising
to what She needed desperately to be broken.

Blame

The night it happened I remember
dirty dishes on the mahogany
and an argument. That means
there'd been company, reason enough.
My father's stupidity, the embarrassment
and Mother holding it in
to dish out later for dessert.

They must have forgotten me
curled in the living room chair, the eye
of the storm drowning herself in a book.
Sunday night. Death rattle of a weekend.

Suddenly a crash. Thud
of a wrecking ball through the roof.
Then silence. A jostling in the hall.
Mother's sharp intake of breath. Then
the screaming. The ceiling over my bed
had fallen, unlocked its slabs: Africa,
Asia, the whole Rand McNally dumping its load
on the small pillow where my head should have been.
The Atlas of ceilings unable to hold anymore.

That was the night of the shrieking
that wouldn't stop and my father's eyes
rummaging in bloodshot for a way out, anywhere
away from her voice shredding over a serrated edge
to trip him. Hadn't he been warned? For a year
plaster bulged over my head like a fat lady
in a hammock, and he, testing, poking at it
with a broom handle. And now,
shuffling backwards in his duck-walk shoes,

yelling *you could have moved the bed,*
why didn't you just move the bed?

What had I done except not be
the thing they could agree on? The eight-year-old
they both saw that night, flat on her back in bed
listening to their harangue before it landed
in a blizzard of broken sidewalks.
Eyes stuck open—pale thing—
staring at the snowflakes of cement.

The Chicken Flag

Route 62.   Virginia.
White two story   on a bend.
Quiet   no sound in sight
except the flag   a flapping square.
Rooster   with a gold fantail
or hen   showing off her yolk.
Maybe a pullet   before the sun.
Or the son.   Shades drawn
in an upstairs room.   A chicken son?
Every family   has a flag.
What's yours?   Two happy bugs?
Four chimpanzees?   One cobra
waiting in a shoe?

Mine is   two dogs
choke-chained   clamped
to each other's   throats
for sixty years.   Canine teeth
for staples   making sure
of the attachment.   First prize
in taxidermy   before it was
disqualified   for being real.
At the bottom   two pups.
Inconsequential.   Call it perfect.
Force it   to be beautiful.
White background.   A black border.
No one can escape.

The Exile

A woman takes the same walk
each afternoon. A three-mile loop
of country road. Clockwise one day,
counterclockwise the next.
Monday her eyes are raised, Tuesday
level, Wednesday down. In six days
she's looked at everything then starts again.

She examines pebbles, acorns. Drops them
and moves on. A cocoon, snails, thistles,
one red feather. Searches through
last year's dump of leaves. Runs her hands
over shelves of fungi. Rummages in ditches
woozy with September—Jewelweed
and pink Lady's Thumbs. Pokes with a stick.

Only the day after late autumn's
first dust of snow when she discovers
a set of footprints running to meet her
does she stop, turn, slip her feet into them,
matching part for part, like Cinderella
stuck to the image of the absent one.

What music does she hear,
swaying between right foot and left,
knuckles ramming a stopper in her mouth?

This is the story of the clarinetist
lost in Ravel's *Bolero*, knowing only
to repeat his one allotted phrase louder
and louder. Violins plucking at their itch.
Mayday Mayday sobbing in the reed.

Forgive and Forget

Like a Swiss army knife the day opened.
Past the Dingo boot factory. Mel's Guns.
The orange highway barriers knocked aside.
Past a dog run over in the third lane.
So I waited. Did my slow dance.
And it came—you.
The curse at the christening.
The proverbial turned-up penny—bad.

Mister Grief, it's been seventeen years.
Was I supposed to forget? Not recognize
your old look under your new look
of fat and receding? Not remember
your best trick: the red cape of charming
dangled in my face until you could
rent out an arena, play the finish to a crowd?

Or did you think I'd forgive, knowing
how you worked it? Passive as a penitent,
hanging around, big-eyed and jittery,
waiting to be saved. The face
you learned to use when a TV evangelist
stole your mother's eyes and she'd yell
Hush and flick her ash. Forget it.

I don't care if deception rocked at the dug.
Smoke and mirrors repents to mirrors and smoke.
I can smell a retread by the flapped-off stink
of rubber on the side of the road. Writing this,
I want you to know, I had to keep the windows open,
the bathroom fan roaring all day long.

The Substitute

The dentist's waiting room was airless,
refugee dust clammy in the drapes
and somewhere a clock.
Four 20-gallon tanks, so algae-covered,
angels were shadows groping in a cave.
His drill, a mantis preying from a hook
and I remember the sound of his shoe
pressing the lever to the floor.
I learned early how to grip a chair,
open up for pain. What did he know
of Novocain? What did I know
of numbers on an arm? I was fourteen.

April 1947. His eyes studying
his right hand—the hooked steel
of his explorer. *I'd like to paint you.*
I pincurled my hair, flipped
my scarf like Doris Day and went.
The white coat that cracked when he leaned,
his tiny mirror neck-bent for sins,
the stiff brush for his hands—gone.
He wore slippers and food stains, bowed
like a maitre d' offering a lady a chair
then squeezed his tubes. The apartment
smelled of yesterday's lunch, of attics,
trunks of baby clothes, camphored dresses
from Russia, a blue feathered hat
saved for Sundays perhaps—a long walk
then tea with crushed raspberries
sucked through a cube of sugar
dissolving between the teeth

like the final sweetness
before Hell began
and Hell's afterlife—a stranger
standing next to a mechanized chair.

He rolled up one sleeve deliberately
as if he wanted me to look, as if
he'd waited years for this, then posed me
seated before a cup of tea. *Tip your head*
he pleaded *the way you used to.*
The clock listened from the other room.
The four aquariums glowed green as a curse
or one of those candles that remembers all night long.

Flying Home

after a visit to my mother

What did she ever want
but to clean house, sing
like Pavarotti with a rag?
New slipcovers, face
at the bottom of the silver bowl.
Then suddenly, the magician
drops a handkerchief and her body
wanders, too small for its skin.
Five feet four to five feet
nothing—the great vanishing
into a pair of house slippers.

What good is understanding
the physiology of spinal disks,
how they crumble like temporary cement?
And what does it matter
knowing all that matters is thrift—the body
huddled around its last nickel of heat
banked for that final conversion?

Dumb Heart, you suck in an old crib,
wanting only what you always wanted.
Look around. Above the clouds
roars a planeload of crying babies.

Crystal

to my sister

Ashes ashes
We all fall down

She's begun to give her things away.
Scarves. What's left of the Limoges.
The 1927 stemware you and I hauled down
once a year to wash, dry, put away.
How silly, we thought, this treasuring
the never used. Such brilliance in braids.
Remember the giddy slippage?
The goblet a year shattered in the sink?

What wouldn't I give to have them back,
last seen forty years ago carried out in garbage.
Tulips cracked from stems, champagne, liqueur.
I think of them, waiting years
in a dark cupboard, upturned mouths
yearning to be touched and sing, etched vines
reaching to catch themselves, *ring around*
a rosy, pocket full of posies and
hold on around the rim.

Today she insists I clean out cabinets,
wash, dry, box up. *Ashes Ashes.*
I tell you, Judy, despite everything,
I'd take Wadsworth Avenue again—toothpick,
spread newspaper, glue—if only to prolong
this moment—she directing in slippers, and I
taking down the gleaming pieces of what's left.

Does that sound too pretty?
All right then, plain as bottle glass
scratched with a nail: I want one more year
before the sink empties, before the suds shatter
skidding toward the hole.

Storage

Earth is the planet of storage.
Any hollow will do. The Hawaiians said
an anguished soul flutters about the body
until scooped up and stoppered in a gourd.
Drags at is more like it. On the day
we decided to put Daddy in the home
he fell three times. His legs, disobedient
as a bundle of sticks. On his knees
facing the chair he fell out of, the seat
chest-high and inaccessible as his mama's lap
gone these thirty years.

I squatted behind him—we who don't speak,
haven't touched for fifty years—shins
at his back for leverage, arms around his chest
locked at the wrists, tugging at dead weight.
Under my pulse, the galley-drum of his heart
banging orders to the rubbery legs, swishing
like so much flotsam on the carpet.

How many times a day do you call 911?
He clawed at the chair's arms, his diaper
slipping off the crack. *Lift me*
he roared. His bald head, face down,
burrowing in the back seam of the chair
as if the fontanel had opened again
and somewhere in that cushion's softness
winked the old keyhole—the wet slit out.

How many times a day? How many an hour?
Now each night I fall asleep like a fish—
eyes open, afraid to close them.
So small. His belongings—
two suitcases next to a strange bed.

Diapers for My Father

Pads or pull-ons—*that*
is the question. Whether to buy
pads dangled from straps
fastened with buttons or Velcro—
pads rising like a bully's cup
stiff as pommel with stickum backs
to stick in briefs. Or, dear God,
the whole thing rubberized,
size 38 in apple green, with
or without elastic leg. Or the kind,
I swear, with an inside pocket
to tuck a penis in—little resume
in a folder. Old mole, weeping
his one eye out at the tunnel's end.

The clerk is nothing but patience
practiced with sympathy.
Her eyes soak up everything.
In ten minutes she's my cotton batting,
my triple panel, triple shield—my Depends
against the hour of the mop: skeleton
with a sponge mouth dry as a grinning brick
waiting in the closet.

She carries my choices to the register,
sighing the floor with each step.
I follow, absorbed away to nothing.

How could Hamlet know what flesh is heir to?
Ask Claudius, panicky in his theft,
hiding in the garden where it all began

or behind the arras, stuffing furbelows
from Gertrude's old court dress into his codpiece.
Or better, ask Ophelia, daughter too
of a foolish, mean-mouthed father,
who launched herself like a boat of blotters
only to be pulled babbling under the runaway stream.

IV. Hunger

The Papaya

for Jean
from a title by Albert Goldbarth

We coveted the one beyond our reach,
the only ripe one, then looked for a stick.
I'll stand on your back or you on mine.
I stand on no one's back, you said.
We laughed—a woman's joke.

As I write this, the children of Elmer, my dead X
who stood on my back worrying his little stick,

his children, mine, are poking sticks in air
on no one's back, pockets open for whatever falls.
Life as piñata tree, fortune-cookie tree. A tree
too heavy with promises like the breadfruit
I saw in Oahu south of where Ferdinand Marcos
lay in state across from the pet cemetery.
South of Mr. Dole's pink plastic pineapple
spewing watered-down juice for tourists.
And the Mormon Temple, all white and beckoning
behind two sets of locked gates, like an exclusive pastry
or one of those official wedding cakes Mussolini built
to sit on top of a boulevard, imitating Heaven
or the Madonna of the Unconditional Lap.

We watched that papaya for a week,
watered at it, imagined the chilled cut halves,
the luxurious first scoop of spoon. And when
it disappeared—plucked or knocked down for need
greater than ours—we looked to the seven remaining ones
huddled together like the alto section of the Vienna Boys Choir,
hiked high and green in their scrotal sacs, not giving an inch.

Hunger

All love has the tug of the first nipple.
Go to Rome. Romulus and Remus
still patty-cake in the shade of a hairy teat
even in public. Soon typewriters will be obsolete
but never that. It's the gold chain
back to the breast pocket, love's first taste
without the sting of salt: rosebud fresh
and wet in the mouth.

The Hawaiians used to say
spirits leave the body through the inner angle
of the eye and return through the feet,
struggling up the body's dark passages.
But I say, love—the singing "Ahhhh"
every tongue depressor's looking for—
makes a home inside the mouth and stays there.
That's why at birth the mouth is readied,
swabbed clean as a foyer. What else
is man's facial hair but welcome mat for more?
A broom sweeping up around love's entrance.

Even at the end, under oxygen,
eyes shut, fingers no more than dried leaves
whispering to the sheets, the mouth
sucking, sucking on the exhausted tongue.

Matisse's Windows

Fishing trawlers two hundred yards out
slosh next to roses in the wallpaper
where a smudge equals the spray
and slap of flounder
as if there were no wall, no dividing brick
between that woman playing solitaire at her table
and boats and bathers in their white caps
and honeymoons.

At night, what fits the hand—cards,
pear, or china cat—abandoned.
It's the window your eyes come back to
where a garden rises blue Jurassic,
and trees, blue as veins
yanked out by the souls at Acheron,
fidget for you beyond the glass.

Only in Nice did he pull the drapes,
drape the parrot cage. Here at last,
the dream of his middle age. Let Pablo get lost
in a jungle of geometry. Here is nothing
but circles: breasts and turbans
and kohl-lined eyes,
lounging in an overstuffed room
so hot you could kiss the moisture
off an upper lip. A male wish. An eleventh hour
wound so bright it reels to look. No night, no day.
No door. Just the woman, waiting.
Her eyes looking out, never wanting to leave.
Her only window—
the man standing in front of her with a brush.

Sunday Morning at the Beach, I Think of Mountains

. . . in images we awake,
Within the very object that we seek.

—Wallace Stevens

I want to write about geography.
Not forests, oceans, or your corner plot.
These change and, like you, ache,
turn, twist into themselves,
send out a periodic flower.

I want to write about the thing
conceived in the chastity above the tree line,
flinging words off its back to clatter
down the slopes, refusing in its nakedness
to be dressed. Perhaps imagination
cannot climb such high reality—
that metaphor for the inaccessible: the ghost
who wears no sheet, the specter
behind the mind's trivia and the heart's stash
whose name's too big to know.

Instead I write what's given—this town
where hedges are gardenia, where sandpipers
tease in baby steps playing Mother-May-I
with the sea. My own failure, taking me
down but not enough so that I struggle
against rising that third and final time.
The mess of love, its appetizer and leftovers
caught in the shark's teeth. And childhood,
how it repeats, pulling on new outfits
as if it traveled through my life

lugging a big suitcase, squeezing me
out of my airplane seat, getting sick in a bag.
And death. And life that is a death: the mossy
yearning of stepping stones across a stream.

But I can't fit a name to the blank gaze of things
whose molecules are hardly stirred to move,
nor can I make up what the tongue
is too clotted to say, or the eyes, like those
of fallen climbers, too unforgiving to bless.

At St. John's Monastery

July 4, 1992

1.

We prefer them medieval—black skirt
and scapular—look away embarrassed
to see beyond where it's marked off-limits
to go—a compound of rose garden with
fountain, lilies and marigold, sprinklers
to keep it young. Here on the 4th they fling
frisbees or polish a golf swing, shouting
like any boys with a ball. I wonder though
which one it was: that one running across
the lawns in sneakers, wearing a baseball
cap, that one reading, or the thoughtful one
in blue, who one night last March, after Mass
when wind rises off the lake looking for
secrets, huddled in the cemetery
crying behind one of the black basalt
stones lined up with the patient others on
the hill. There, he took from his sleeve a poem
copied from a slim book, then—kiss first—placed
a small, bronze bas-relief, two inches high,
maybe his mother had, when he was five,
given (it was so small) of Mary and
the Child joined on her lap but each looking
out and away, for what if they turned and
saw each other's eyes hopeless, or, like him,
saw through another's eyes Love's love-knot turned
love not, turned weed, dogbane and common, what
to him was purple, royal in the fields?

2.

[The new style of poetry reads flat as a floor.
Lines identically tongued & machine grooved.
Floors for a gym or highway.
No splinters no scratches no scars. Over them
fast, and who cares
if it's Duluth or San Bernardino?
It's two gas stations & a Red Roof Inn.

I'd like to tell this story in a canoe
with you listening at the other end. A cove
where the lake stops in a tangle of lily
thick as carpet over a moving floor—
so intricately woven you're pulled to walk it. And there
if we see a flower opening its white cup, you or I
might say *chalice* and no one would blush.]

3.

Like a chalice he brought his gifts, walking
hunched over from the cold, between double
lines of young trees kept in wire cages. He
wasn't young. Neither was the one beneath
the stone. Fifty-seven and three years gone.
Above him, blue spruce waved limbs, dragonish,
and he saw how the blue was just the ends,
the center limbs bare, pushing nourishment
like a toothless mother out to the young.
He thought of Mother Church and Saint Benedict:
To each one as he had need. And he knew
himself—hungry.
                What say we here,
white lily on a lake, when the line breaks,
when tongues fail? For what does a human tree
say, caged thirty years to keep it straight and

saved? And saved from what, except another
like him—a hart, perhaps, soft-eyed, nibbling
at the first green shoots? Instead, his hunger
served as augury: a caged tree rustling of
a Bliss where Love's purple is dished out in
feasts of flesh: wages for those who, yes, lived
like a weed, shriveling in a closed-up house.

4.

Resurrection will ring from the east.
The graves will kick open and they
Will swing up on their heels—
The good boys in their black cassocks—
And stand in rows like new school pencils
Red-faced before the sun.

Bells will melt.
The playing fields will be left behind.
And carved on their chests as on their
Basalt blocks, their God name, Brother name,
Glory name. On the back, the old name
Mother waved to from the stands.

All is ready. The rows of young aspen
Are locked in their cages—those nervous trees.
Ecce signum. Behold the sign.
The boys are lined up in their slings, clutching
Their beads, rigged up to the sad catapults.

Confession

She awakens into her next life.
The present suddenly foreign
yet endearing as if it were
her grandmother's hairbrush she found
in her hand, the silver handle tarnished,
her own hairs in the yellowed bristles.

Across the street, the cathedral's
great bronze bells open their mouths, clang
to make her say it, write it, harsh
and simple: *I have failed.*
But the pen stalls. Had she not been
rocked, the tortured rope yanked enough
to make the tongue admit, plain,
the truth—that her old life
gave birth to this, the way a crescent moon
grows its murderer in its arms?

What she wanted was to write like a cellist,
leaning over the sloped shoulder, coaxing
out of the wooden life between her legs—
the form's amnesia: the sealed kiss of the ax,
still stuck, shuddering in the heartwood.

But even this morning, the sun holding up
the old world's face like a chin strap,
she can't hide from herself what the ink
knows before it's risked: out of *the rag
and bone shop of the heart* her ladder
turned out to be a footstool, and her joy,
scraping on strings with a peeled stick.

Letter from an Empty House

to Bruce

Footsteps glide the floorboards
of this house, and noiseless dishes
gather in the sink. Even you, Peacock,
singe my dreams then burn away. Outside
wild turkeys peck at slugs, and gnats
float like flocks in air as Keats said
or were they buds?
and is it Shelley? (no matter) He's filled
the vacant house in Hampstead Heath
with Fanny's voice and Fanny's shine and look—
a pounded pillow with a stain.
Nothing's empty long.
The outside's ruckus and decay
corkscrew through the screens. If not,
impatient, we hang our vacancy out of doors
or spread it like a cloth upon the ground.
"Springes to catch woodcocks" Will said.
A magician's trick, plucking from emptiness.
Rabbits out of hats. White doves from chaos.
And since for now I count me lucky, Peacock, this.

White River

Creative life . . . the river
beneath the river.

—Clarissa Pinkola Estés

Today walking to the river
I saw twelve silent hearts
Dangled above a porch swing.
Six pairs of lovers, so close they overlapped.
But it's wind that makes wind chimes clap
And sing. I count on the river. It knows
Where it's going, races to get there.

Even in January, I lead my footprints
To watch the water wrestle down ice
The way a Siamese twin
Struggles with his other half, the one
Who wants to die. But now, June,
And the river's hearts sing on a string.

A willow bends to touch it. *Wait for me*
Wait for me the willow weeps
Thrashing arms like fire, tugging
At the roots knotted in mud like a woman
Reduced to arguing with her own veins—
Doing this for years.

Behind me I hear voices.
A man and a young girl.
I don't turn around. I want him
To be her father explaining: the wind chimes
Or the tree, and then the river—how

Even in summer, sequined crawl or quick
Black slide over rocks, the river flings back
An afterthought, what looks like regret.
Show her that too—
All those white handkerchiefs saying goodbye.

Under Water

There is no bottom
To the bottom of this world.
The wind grieves oceanic. And limbs
Of the sixty-foot spruce darkening my window
Grope restless as eelgrass or the swaying
Tentacles of Salome, liquid in her veils.
You know that story. John the waterboy
Lost his head to her. And she,
Stuck forever in the dance—two feet
Jammed into one shoe.
Punishment enough for anybody.

Imagine each year of your life
Like that. A fever of telephone poles.
A string of paper dolls. Of showgirls
Wearing two dimes and a nickel, imitating
Columns screwed into the stairs.
Even the Rockettes, New York's row of hearts—
Pistons for knees, jumpy as jackhammers,
Kicking in place toward no place at all.

Days like this I understand
Why women are pulled to water, walk the beach
Watching like Easter Island mysteries
As if the sea were a melt of crystal ball
Or a lady's mirror leaky with yearning.

A wise woman covers her mirrors.
What sign can be hoped for?
The moon walks pulling a silver leash,
And the old sea, that mother, that bitch
Long in the tooth and foaming in her collar, heels.

From the Looking Glass

Forgive yourself the droop, the direction
Down. Forgive the folds, lines, your mother's hands
Thrust from your cuffs—her blue-veined gift—their fan
Of bones, fragile under papery skin.
Forgive the skin, loose between fingers, shirred
Silk from an old shirt, turkey neck, out of
Style—that sin. Tell me, whose hurt would you cup
In your two hands for its bright self brought down,
If *your* collection—that old upheaval
Of sheets, the wrenched cry of knee to knee, skin's
Three-time stretch over a pregnant hill—this
Landfill—is let go now, comfortless, bent,
Reaching for ground, the rose-tipped breasts hanging
In air, hardened shut by such cold clanging?

Unfinished Lines

Chasing an updraft, the snow defies gravity
While across the street, smoke from a gray house
Pushes its way in between . . .

Inside the back cover of Stevens' *Collected Poems*,
snow blows wild, covering the blank page
with whiteness, while smoke snakes its way
between the cold mysteries. What couldn't I see
nine years ago looking out that hospital window
before recovery, before the end of the Cold War,
before George Bush or rap music or today's
hazy Minnesota afternoon, to finish those lines?

Today, outside this window, leaves are dancing
their one July, fat from last night's rain
that fell the way it fell in Eden. (The smoke
persists, pulls like a clue.) For what?
And why today do I remember the old man
down that hospital corridor—trussed up in tubes,
turned every two hours, the mattress raised and
lowered to rock the blood—a sour bundle of breathing
gone yellow, the whole family back each night,
flipping pages of their magazines,
taking turns practicing (for they would need to know)
the words of grief, "Ah, but it was better so."

So we remain. Even his arthritic plant
giving up on the sill, and me, a green robe
wandering the corridors, enamored by a snow
struggling against falling, and a scribble of smoke
that will spend nine years holding us, trying in coils
to find some other way, as if there were one,
in between.

Poem for Trees

Did you ever notice how trees don't touch
even when dropping pods or flinging seed
or landing them in helicopters like a private joke?
They sense each other's presence, lean away,
grow a limb only where there's room.

Leaves gossip tree to tree, but leaves
are young. In October, young to dying.
Out of work, shiftless, each one a gold watch.
They grab on, ancient mariners—desperate
for time beyond the rake, the plastic bag
twist-tied at the curb.

Only the bald body maintains
a separateness, a fort, a steady tick-tock
through the hundred years of its labors.

What fantasy is it that wishes otherwise?
That underground, the earth is not
just cemetery. That roots inch,
searching like moles, for miles, years.
That maybe in my backyard, the taproot
of the Japanese Maple that grows by the pagoda
of the Great Bonze has found my Sweetgum at last
and they lie like snakes together, touching
all along each other's length, quiet and breathing.